Bridget McNulty is a writer, content strategist and co-founder of Sweet Life, South Africa's largest online diabetes community.

She lives in Cape Town, South Africa, with her husband, son and daughter, and loves nothing more than a cup of tea and a good book – preferably somewhere green and leafy.

Find out more at www.bridgetmcnulty.com

The
Grief
Handbook

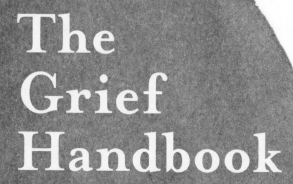

The Grief Handbook

A guide through the worst days of your life

Bridget McNulty

WATKINS

Sharing Wisdom Since 1893

This edition first published in the UK and USA in 2021 by
Watkins, an imprint of Watkins Media Limited
Unit 11, Shepperton House
89-93 Shepperton Road
London
N1 3DF

enquiries@watkinspublishing.com

Illustrations by Lauren Fowler

10 9 8 7 6 5 4 3 2 1

Designed and typeset by JCS Publishing Service Ltd

Printed and bound in the United Kingdom by TJ Books Ltd.

A CIP record for this book is available from the British Library

ISBN: 978-1-78678-58 (paperback)
ISBN: 978-1-78678-535-0 (eBook)

www.watkinspublishing.com

Contents

Hello

Welcome. I'm so sorry you're here. If there's one thing we can all be certain of in life, it's that we will, one day, have to lose someone we love: it's the price we pay for that love. But that doesn't make it any easier. Before you read any further, I want you to know that this is a safe space to feel whatever it is that you are feeling. You can be angry or sad or anxious or bereft or lost or disbelieving or any other emotion you find coming your way. It's all okay. It's all normal. It all sucks.

Grief is such a strange thing. It is the most universal experience – the one thing that unites us all, regardless of where we live or who we are, no matter our culture or colour or beliefs. And yet, at the same time, it is the most unique and personal experience, because no two people grieve in the same way. Grief affects every part of us: the way we feel, the way we think, our physical and mental health, the way we breathe and carry ourselves in the world.

Yet humans are not good at grief. How is that possible? We don't know what to say, how to act or what to do when someone dies. As a result, it can feel as if it's up to the grieving person to "get over it" as quickly as possible, to spare the social discomfort. Please don't. Take as much time and be as visibly upset as you need to be – other people will adjust. There is, in fact, definitive proof that grief is one of the worst things that can happen to you: the Holmes and Rahe Stress Scale lists the top ten most stressful life events, and death of a spouse or child and death of a close family member are in the top five. This is literally one of the hardest things you will ever have to face.

Add in Covid-19 and things become even more difficult. On top of grief being a personal, physical, mental assault, many people are having to deal with not being able to say goodbye to the person they love, or not being able to honour them with a funeral, or mourning multiple losses at the same time. It feels like the whole world is grieving, but we don't know what to do.

I am not a grief expert. However, I have a few suggestions: things that helped me when I was feeling desperate. Silly things like colouring in that reminded me I could still make something beautiful in the midst of my sadness. Inspiring things like poems or wise words from those who have walked before us on this bleak path. Activities to hopefully unlock some of the sadness and let it out into the world. Throughout this book, I've highlighted grief experts who have cast some light on my journey, in the hope that they might cast some on yours.

What I do know for sure is that the only way out is through: it is a choice to face your grief head-on, in a conscious way, or to deny it and stay stuck. It's obvious which path I think is the more helpful choice … I hope this book will help you to take the first few steps.

∞

My grief journey hit me sideways, out of nowhere. My mum – my best friend – was a healthy 72-year-old until she started complaining of weird symptoms: sore feet and acid reflux, mainly. She changed her diet, went to the podiatrist, but the weird symptoms kept coming. When she suddenly lost weight and started sleeping more, we sent her to a specialist physician. She was diagnosed with cancer and died 13 days later.

My dad, my three elder brothers and I all grieved differently. That's one thing you learn very quickly: there is no right or wrong way to grieve, and everyone has their own style. Whatever you are doing is totally fine, and totally normal, and absolutely right for you right now (even if other people don't understand it). One of my brothers busied himself with work, one sat by my mum's bedside every day, one was forced to focus on his children. I became hyper-organized, as if keeping the wheels turning in the house would somehow reverse the awful events that were happening around us.

And they were so awful – the kind of awful that I would have found far-fetched in a movie. The day we brought my mum home from the hospital, earth movers and a wrecking ball rolled up the driveway of the neighbouring house and began to demolish it. We watched a house that had stood next to our childhood home for 30 years being smashed to pieces as they ripped up mature trees from the earth and left a desolate wasteland in their wake. A bit heavy-handed on the symbolism, don't you think?

At the same time, one of my nieces ended up in hospital for six days, unable to stop vomiting. All the kids (five, in total) caught a vicious stomach bug. My mum's dog committed suicide by jumping in the pool and drowning (even though she could swim). Then a week after we brought my mum home, she died – just like that.

∞

In the quiet that followed this storm, I tried to find solace. I'm a reader, so I looked for books that could shine a light through the fog of grief I found myself in. But everything I read was either too dense and philosophical or presumed I wanted a religious interpretation of death and grief, which I didn't.

What I wanted was an honest exploration of how to deal with the worst thing. I wanted short, succinct explanations of what grief is and how to survive it, some space to be really angry and really sad and channel that in some way, and some words of inspiration to get me through the darkest days. I wanted a handbook: literally a hand to lead me through my grief. I couldn't find it, so I wrote it. I really hope it helps in some small way.

I know it can be tempting to distract yourself out of grief. I know that letting all the pain and heartache and fury out can feel scary. Yet I also know that grief denied does not disappear: it merely cloaks itself in a disguise for another day. If you are able to, I really encourage you to let it all out now – when it's fresh and raw, and appropriate. Take advantage of this moment and this book. Nobody will ever see what you write down.

I also want to encourage you to reach out and ask for support if you need it. Grief is natural and inevitable. But it's also a close cousin of depression, and reaching for a hand to help you through the worst days can make all the difference. If you don't feel like you're coping, some resources that might be helpful are listed at the end of the book. The most important thing at the moment is to get through each day, whatever that looks like. One step at a time.

I am so sorry to be meeting you at this awful time. I promise you that one day it will feel a bit better – this too, like everything else, shall pass.

All my love,
Bridget

Colour me in ...

THE EARLY DAYS

Shock and disbelief

One of the things I found hardest to deal with in the weeks and months after my mum died was the disbelief that she had gone. It seemed impossible that the world could continue as if nothing had happened when I no longer had a mum.

Part of this, of course, was shock – and I think shock is inherent in any death, even those that have been anticipated for some time. The sudden reality of someone who was alive and who then stops breathing – forever – is too harsh a disjunction not to be accompanied by shock. Along with this disbelief came another, uglier, feeling though. It felt as if the world had tilted on its axis and something was *wrong*. Not just a little bit wrong, but "call the manager, we need to fix this" wrong.

I would walk around looking at older women and mentally calculate their age. If they looked older than my mum, I would get inexplicably angry at them for still being alive when she wasn't. If I saw a mother and daughter having coffee together, or walking down the street, I shot them dirty looks. I thought of all the people I knew who have troubled relationships with their mums, and wondered why they couldn't have drawn the short straw instead of me. My dad kept telling me he felt cheated out of a decade with her, and that made my heart crumble, over and over again.

Of course, when we're feeling rational we know that death is not unfair. It is the one equalizer, in fact – the one thing that every single person (you and me included) is guaranteed of in this life. But the specific death of *my* mum continued to feel unfair for months. It was such an easy spiral to go down, too – I'd see a pair of earrings my mum bought me and think, "Who's going to buy me earrings now?" and then quickly segue into, "Nobody loved buying me gifts as much as my mum", and "Nobody loved me the way my mum loved me", and "I will never have a mum again". And let me tell you, picking yourself up off the floor when you start your morning choosing a pair of earrings and end in, "I will never have a mum again", is a hard task.

My advice, if you care to take it (please feel free not to) is *not* to press on the bruise. There are so many little things that hurt every day, and you can either press on them and follow them to their desperately sad conclusions or consciously resist that urge. Especially in these first few weeks, don't go down that path. There is plenty of time to think all of those thoughts, and I promise they will come back to you. However, give yourself some time to recover from the shock before you start processing all the big truths about your life right now – and forever after.

I would go so far as to suggest that you think up some rules of survival for yourself for the first few weeks, while you're coming to terms with your loss. Here are a few that helped me:

1. Treat yourself gently

Really gently. Think of a newborn baby, or an injured bird. You have just been through the worst thing, and you continue to live through the worst thing. Cut yourself some slack. This is true emotionally, of course, but I think it's also true physically. I found it really comforting to wear soft clothing and cosy slippers. I started sleeping with my childhood teddy bear again after decades of pretending to be a grown-up. I lay down and read a lot. I drank a lot of tea. Comfort will look and feel different for you, but I really encourage you to do whatever you can to make yourself feel nurtured and loved.

2. No late nights

When grief knocks, routine goes out the window. It suddenly seems okay to stay up till all hours and sleep in, to shuffle around in pyjamas and eat junk food all the time. The trouble with all of these behaviours is that they don't necessarily make you feel better, and some – like late nights – can make you feel much worse.

There's something about the quiet and still of night-time that brings all the hardest, worst feelings to the fore. This is not the time for emotional conversations or quiet introspection. Rather, put yourself to bed at a normal hour and try to treat your body the way you know it likes to be treated. Eating junk food feels good in the moment, but rarely feels good half an hour later, and you need to be treating your body as kindly as possible.

One of my dad's friends gave him the most practical advice related to this: eat meals at normal times. Even if you're not hungry and not interested, eat as if you're a normal person who needs breakfast, lunch and dinner at regular times. It helps.

3. Move your body

Which brings me to the next point: move your body. Exercise may be the last thing you feel like doing – it was for me. But on days that I could drag myself out for a walk around the block, I felt so much better. That was literally all I could muster – a slow walk – but the combination of movement and fresh air did very good things for my psyche. Try to find the easiest possible movement you can do regularly, and keep at it.

4. Don't question your feelings

Whatever you're feeling is totally fine. You might be feeling okay or desperate or depressed or angry, or any number of other emotions. It is all totally fine. There is no right or wrong way to do grief – I'll keep saying it – so don't question your feelings or worry that you're doing it wrong, or that what you're feeling isn't normal. There is no normal in this. It is all so hard.

ADVICE

Psychotherapist and author Esther Perel has written extensively about how to cope with the relationship aspect of separation and grief during Covid-19. Her advice for "small, rapid interventions" is just as useful if you're grieving the loss of someone you love.

- Pay attention to what you're paying attention to: news, arguments, and otherwise.

- Get outside the best you can.

- Short term strategies start in your body; a bodied-up ritual involving breathing and stretching will help you relax and restore.

- Reassure yourself that you are okay right now.

- Focus on one breath at a time.

- Know that thriving doesn't always mean being productive.

What's helpful to remember is that you don't have to do it all at once. Try to adjust your expectations to one day at a time – or half a day at a time, or one hour at a time. Whatever gets you through the next little bit.

On the flip side, if you're feeling surprisingly fine – that's okay too. Everyone grieves at different speeds. It may hit you a few weeks or months later. It may be years later, in a seemingly unrelated incident, or over a lesser grief that links to this one. There are no rules when it comes to grieving the people we have lost, no regulations on how to do it right. You do you.

THINGS TO REMEMBER DURING THE FIRST FEW WEEKS:

1. Treat yourself gently

2. No late nights

3. Move your body

4. Don't question your feelings

What are your rules of survival?

_____

_____

_____

_____

_____

_____

_____

_____

_____

_____

The fog of grief

Probably the most helpful concept for me, in those hard and confusing first days and weeks after my mum's death, was understanding the fog of grief. This isn't just an idea, but a reality. If you find yourself feeling tired all the time (no matter how much you sleep), that's the fog of grief. If you're suddenly clumsy and tripping on things that have always been there, or dropping cups or plates for no reason, that's the fog of grief. If you can't remember the three things you had to buy at the store, or keep forgetting meetings or coffee dates, that's the fog of grief.

Essentially, the fog of grief is a deep cloud that descends over your life for a while (weeks or months) and makes it hard to function. It has both an emotional component, in that you feel sad or anxious or tired, and a physical one – the clumsiness, the forgetfulness, a deep exhaustion. You might feel physically unwell, too, with frequent stomach aches or headaches or a persistent fluey feeling. This is all totally normal (and totally sucky).

> *"Grief causes a fog to roll into our lives. The fog of grief can affect our ability to think or concentrate. This fog often sets in right after a loved one has died. But even after the shock wears off, the fog can linger or come and go for a long time … What happens is that our grief gets so heavy that it surrounds us, clouds our minds, and interferes with our ability to think clearly. We're on overload."*
> Kenneth C Haugk, *Journeying Through Grief*, Book 1, page 27

ADVICE

A friend gave me Kenneth C Haugk's series
of four books, *Journeying Through Grief,*
one by one during the first year. Haugk is a
psychologist, author, pastor and teacher, and
while I found much of his writing too religious,
this idea of the fog of grief was like someone
lighting a candle in a dark room. I immediately
took a photo of the page and sent it to my
brothers and my dad, all of whom had been
going through the same thing. It was such a
relief to put a name to the feeling and to know
that I wasn't permanently damaged. A part
of me had worried that this was just what life
without my mum would be like: confusing,
tiring, forgetful.

Because our emotions are overloaded – maxed
out on grief – there's no space for anything
else. I remember feeling as if I was already
80 per cent full of emotion, so any little thing
tipped me over the edge. I literally could not
watch or read anything that wasn't a comedy:
the merest hint of drama or real life made me
cry. I subsisted on a diet of romantic comedies
and sitcoms.

∞

When you're in the fog of grief, it can feel like you're just going through the motions, doing the things that you know are expected of you because they're expected of you, but with no involvement in them. It's almost as if you're playing the part of who you used to be, but all the heart has gone out of your performance.

I felt as if every morning when I woke up I (involuntarily) picked up a heavy backpack of emotion and carried it through the day. It was exhausting. The fog was mental (my brain was on a go-slow) and physical (I felt as if I was moving through mud) and emotional (everything was heavy and murky).

I remember when I was in the thickest part of the fog that I would wake up in the morning and think: "Okay, let's do this. Get up, eat breakfast, make breakfast and pack lunch boxes for the kids. Then have a shower, go to work, come home, play with the kids, make dinner, watch TV, go to bed." It was a laundry list of things I had to do to get through the day – and this included seeing friends and exercising and eating healthy food – because I knew (on some level) that it was important. Yet I couldn't *feel* it. I was just going through the motions.

I will say that having kids and grieving is a terrible combination. Terrible in the original meaning of the word: both awful and powerful. Awful because kids are so profoundly self-centred that they find it impossible to empathize for more than a few minutes. My son was almost five and my daughter not yet three when my mum died, and although they are very sweet, affectionate children, they could not understand how I was still sad after a week or two. "Are you sad?" became a frequent question if my voice didn't sound right or I said I was tired and didn't want to play. If I replied in the affirmative, it was quickly followed by, "Why?" Let me tell you, having to repeat over and over again, "Because my mum died," is not an easy way to get through the afternoon.

At the same time, and in exact counterbalance to that, having kids forced me into a healthy routine. Every morning when I woke up, all I wanted to do was roll over and go back to sleep. I didn't care what I ate, I didn't care what I wore, I didn't care if I interacted with the world at all. But my kids cared: they wanted real food and for me to take them to school wearing real clothes (not pyjamas). They wanted their mum, and so I had to rise above what I was feeling and be a mum. Some days this felt like too much to ask for. On the rare occasion I got an evening to myself, I totally succumbed to what life would have been like without kids: watching romantic comedies while eating whatever I felt like (*Sleepless in Seattle* and a whole punnet of mushrooms fried in butter and eaten straight from the pan, if you must know).

My laundry list of things I had to do to get through the day was largely centred on what I couldn't escape: I have Type 1 diabetes, so I have to eat regularly. I have kids, so I have to feed them. They won't let me lie down and read, so I have to play with them. However, this sense of duty also ensured that I didn't get too mired in the fog of grief … It kept me moving forward, no matter how reluctantly.

If you're in the thick of this fog at the moment, I see you. It is so hard. It feels like it will never end. These are the worst days.

But in the midst of all this, there are some things you have to get out of bed for – some duties you have to fulfil. What are those? Writing them down not only helps clarify what you need to focus on, but it lets you off the hook for all the things you don't need to pay attention to. Just focus on what has to be done for now: you're in survival mode, and so you should be.

MY LAUNDRY LIST:

At the same time, give yourself the space to recognize that there are some big gaps in your life now: some key roles that your loved one filled that are now vacant. My mum was my number one cheerleader: the one person I could call with any triumph, big or small. "I got a fantastic discount on Tupperware!" "I'm being interviewed on TV!" "I didn't snap when the kids whined!" No matter how insignificant the detail, she wanted to hear it, and celebrate me, and I never felt like I was boasting or looking for praise. She also cared deeply about – and remembered – all the minor details in my life. "How did that recipe turn out?" "Did you get a better night's sleep last night?" "Are your new shoes giving you blisters?"

Nobody in my life currently cares to that level of detail, and oh, I miss it! I have found replacements for most of her other roles – one of my friends plugs a gap here, another there, my husband that one and my brothers the ones over there. But there are some things I just miss. What do you miss most?

WHAT I'LL MISS MOST:

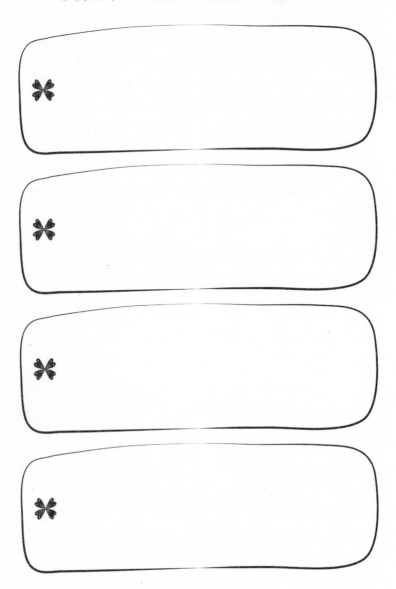

The inadequacy of words

I'm a writer and a reader, so words have always been my friends. I take an unnecessary amount of pride in my vocabulary (even if I can't always pronounce the words). So it was a real blow when I realized that there are not enough words for grief.

The trouble is, of course, that we've used the words before, when things weren't nearly so bad. The fog of grief is difficult to explain because the only words we have at our disposal don't feel weighty enough. I would often tell people that I felt sad and exhausted. Yet neither "sad" nor "exhausted" was big enough for what I was feeling: it was a sadness that seeped into every cell of my body, a bone-weary exhaustion that made every action an effort.

Similarly, "heartbroken", "grief-stricken", "depressed" – they're all part of daily life. They don't encapsulate the weight and depth of emotion that grief brings, and leaves behind.

One of the hardest things about grieving is that it's not a linear process: you don't start it, tick off the boxes and get to the end. It's cyclical. So you start feeling better and then you find yourself right back where you started – triggered by something seemingly harmless or reminded of your grief by the date or the weather or the perfume a stranger is wearing as they walk past you. And then you're back in the depths of it. With no words to describe how awful you feel that haven't been said so many times before.

ADVICE

"Grief is the least linear thing I know."

Jan Richardson is an ordained minister, an artist and a writer. Her version of religion feels very welcoming – she invites you to join her if you would like to and leaves space for you to take what you need from her wisdom. Her husband died suddenly in 2013, and she writes beautifully about grief and how to navigate it.

"I've been thinking lately about how grief is full of hidden rooms. And some of those rooms hold explosives, and some of those rooms hold treasures, and we don't know quite what we're going to get when we open the door, or when the doors open for us. That's how grief works: it comes on us not by choice, typically, and not something we would have willingly opened the door to, not something we would have chosen to welcome in."

Jan Richardson,
The Painted Prayerbook

This can be a really lonely place, too. Up until my mum died, I had always been able to find the words to describe how I felt (sometimes painstakingly so). Now there is a gulf between my feelings and being able to express them. It feels achingly lonely, like the rest of the world suddenly doesn't speak my language and can't possibly understand where I'm coming from.

How do you feel today, do you know? Sometimes finding the right word can be a balm – being able to pinpoint precisely where you are on an emotional map feels reassuring, somehow. Here's a space to try out words for feelings and see if they fit – feel free to add your own if they don't.

TODAY I FEEL...

foggy

okay

exhausted

sad

guilty

down

lost

empty

confused

lonely

impatient

irritable

betrayed

regretful

nervous

stuck

tired

fine

bereft

poorly

angry

well

forlorn

hopeless

heartbroken

anxious

The pit of grief

After a few rounds, I came to recognize this cycle as falling into a pit of grief. I would be walking along, feeling okay (not good, but okay) and then I would suddenly feel the earth sloping away underneath my feet. Before I knew it I was back in the pit of grief. Sometimes I could identify the trigger right away, sometimes it felt as if I woke up in the pit without any conscious thought. Perhaps the two are combined – you don't notice the pit coming because the fog of grief is so thick.

Either way, my point is this:

- Be easy on yourself.
- Be kind to yourself.
- If you do stupid things or have dumb accidents or forget something you've known for years, don't beat yourself up about it.
- The fog of grief is real and hard and all-consuming.
- But it passes ... eventually.

It's not necessarily any easier because you've lived through this feeling before – the only consolation is that you know,

now, that the fog does eventually lift. It's not your first time at this rodeo.

This is why the general life advice is not to make any big decisions in the six months following the death of a loved one: your brain isn't connected properly. It can be tempting to make a big change like moving house or city because it feels like there are just too many memories surrounding you where you are now, but it's safer to postpone those kinds of decisions until the fog of grief has lifted – anything irreversible should wait six months (or a year). If you think about it, all those potential changes are actually very stressful in themselves: moving house, switching jobs, ending a relationship. And if there's one thing you don't need at the moment, it's more stress. What can help is to honour those impulses by writing them down – writing a letter to your future self outlining what you want to do. In six months (or a year), look back at this letter and decide if you still feel the same way. By then, the feelings will have had a chance to percolate; they won't be knee-jerk reactions to the pain or desperate attempts to change the scenery.

Your only job, for this first year, is to get through it. That's it. You don't have to conquer your grief or create anything beautiful out of it, or bounce back or any of that nonsense. You just need to endure.

I know it feels as if you'll never get your brain back or feel halfway normal again. But I promise the fog of grief will pass. For now, try to distract yourself, get through every day, keep breathing.

You can do it, I promise.

DEAR FUTURE SELF,

_____

_____

_____

_____

_____

_____

_____

_____

_____

_____

_____

_____

_____

_____

_____

_____

_____

_____

_____

DATE: _____

DISTRACTIONS:

* Watch a movie

* Go for a walk

* Bake something

* Try out a new recipe for dinner

* Go out for a drink/coffee with a friend

* Do some exercise

* Watch a funny TV show

* Meditate

Real life doesn't stop

In those first few terrible weeks, I had the opening lines of
W H Auden's poem running through my mind on repeat:

> *Stop all the clocks, cut off the telephone,*
> *Prevent the dog from barking with a juicy bone,*
> *Silence the pianos and with muffled drum*
> *Bring out the coffin, let the mourners come.*
>
> W H Auden, "Funeral Blues (Stop All
> the Clocks)", *The Year's Poetry*, 1938

But of course in real life none of that happens. You get
a week or two off work (if you're lucky) and then the
arbitrarily agreed-upon three months of mourning, and
then? It seems like it's time to slap on a smile and get on
with things.

Real life doesn't stop and tragedy doesn't skirt you just
because you're deep in grief.

∞

Six weeks (almost to the day) after my mum died, my
husband left for work on his motorbike, as he did every day.
Five minutes later, I got a message: *Just been hit by a car.*

After the avalanche of worst-case scenarios that we had just
lived through, I didn't dare to hope or worry until I saw
him, lying on the side of the road, unable to be moved for

fear his back was broken. And it was, although not badly (thank heavens). His wrist was also fractured, and for the next four months he couldn't drive.

More immediately, we spent the day in a hospital where the bleeping of the machines made it hard for me to breathe. Back at home, I had to sponge bath him, as I had been sponge bathing my dying mum six weeks before. I had to wake in the night to help him turn and give him pain medication, as I'd been doing for my mum.

I had to check him into hospital for a routine surgery that didn't feel routine because the hospital looked and smelled exactly the same as the one in which my mum had been diagnosed with four different kinds of cancer.

I was back to being the nurse, and the primary caregiver for our kids.

My grief was put on hold.

I have since learnt that experiences like this fall into something called "complicated grief", where the grief journey is not straightforward. It might be a second incident, like my husband's accident, or the situation surrounding your loved one's death (Covid-19, suicide, murder, an accident, anything that feels out of the "normal" natural rhythm of life).

What is complicated grief?

Sometimes, despite your best efforts, grief doesn't pass.
Those first painful months persist and life continues
to feel hopeless and meaningless. There's no gradual
lightening of despair, no easing of the pain. This is known
as complicated grief. As Dr Kathy Shear, the Founder and
Director of the Center for Complicated Grief, explains:

> *"People with complicated grief don't know what's wrong.
> They assume that their lives have been irreparably
> damaged by their loss and cannot imagine how they can
> ever feel better. Grief dominates their thoughts and feelings
> with no respite in sight."*
>
> Dr Kathy Shear, "Complicated Grief Overview", 2015

What are the signs of complicated grief?

1. **Relentless troubling thoughts:** Feeling caught up
   in disturbing and unsettling thoughts of how things
   could have worked out differently.

2. **Avoidance of potential triggers:** Doing whatever is
   necessary to avoid reminders of the loss or things that
   might trigger negative emotions.

3. **Inability to be distracted:** Finding it difficult or impossible to unplug from the painful emotions of grief or to take a break or find distraction.

What might influence complicated grief?

It's a strange term – "complicated grief" – because it naturally suggests that the other kind of grief is simple, and we all know that isn't the case. But there are certain things that can contribute to a more complex grief journey. If your loved one died suddenly, in a particularly traumatic way, or if they were young, that is inevitably more difficult than if they were old and in poor health. If another stressful life incident happens too soon after their death, that can lead to complicated grief. Just as an earthquake has second tremors that can add to the devastation, this second stressful life event can make the journey of grief more difficult.

And of course, if you weren't able to say goodbye properly – as is the case with so many Covid-19 deaths – that certainly makes things more difficult and complicated.

How do you get help for complicated grief?

Don't try to go it alone. Reach out for help – to a grief counsellor or certified therapist. Dr Shear has developed a short-term therapy called complicated grief therapy (CGT), with the strongest evidence base of any grief treatment in the world. You can find out more about it on the Center for Complicated Grief's website (see the "Grief resources" section).

∞

At the time, I didn't know what to do, so I just kept trudging on. In retrospect, perhaps I should have asked for help. What can I say?

It was excruciatingly hard.

It felt like bone grating on bone, every day.

I could feel the grief burning me from the inside, but there was literally no space or time for me to give it attention.

I have since discovered that my experience – my mum dying so suddenly, with me right beside her the whole time, my husband being hit by a car – could be classified as trauma. Not being able to breathe as I walked down the hospital corridor may have been a sign of post-traumatic stress disorder (PTSD). I don't know about you, but when I hear the words "trauma" and "PTSD" I immediately think of war veterans … I didn't think it was possible for me to experience trauma, in my safe, comfortable daily life. Yet once I started digging deeper, so much of it resonated with me.

> *"We have learned that trauma is not just an event that took place sometime in the past; it is also the imprint left by that experience on mind, brain, and body. This imprint has ongoing consequences for how the human organism manages to survive in the present."*
> Dr Bessel van der Kolk, *The Body Keeps the Score: Mind, Brain and Body in the Healing of Trauma*, 2015

ADVICE

What's fascinating about Dr van der Kolk's many years of research into trauma is that he has proven – with scientific studies – that trauma isn't just the single (or repeated) event that happened. It is an imprint left by that experience on your mind, your brain and your body – most of all your body. Your body physically continues to feel as if the trauma is happening now.

So if you want to be able to move past the trauma, your body needs to learn that the danger has passed, that it's safe to live in the reality of the present. This isn't something you can figure out on your own: it requires guidance and professional help. If you've experienced trauma, you are not alone – there are tools that can help you through this.

What is PTSD?

"Post-traumatic stress disorder (PTSD) is a type of anxiety disorder which you may develop after being involved in, or witnessing, traumatic events."

www.mind.org.uk

One in eleven people will be diagnosed with PTSD in their lifetime, and women are twice as likely as men to have PTSD (American Psychiatric Organization: www.psychiatry. org). It is far more common than many of us realize.

What are the symptoms of PTSD?
According to the American Psychiatric Organization, there are four categories of symptoms of PTSD, as well as some physical symptoms.

1. **Intrusion:** Memories that you can't shake, disturbing dreams or flashbacks.

2. **Avoidance:** Not wanting to talk (or think) about what happened, and avoiding any potential reminders of the event that could be a trigger.

3. **Alterations in cognition and mood:** Not being able to remember things about what happened, negative thoughts and feelings about what happened and who was to blame, ongoing fear, horror, anger, guilt or shame, and feeling unable to enjoy things, people or positive emotions.

4. **Alterations in arousal and reactivity:** Trouble concentrating or sleeping, being easily triggered to anger or easily startled, feeling overly suspicious or behaving recklessly.

Physical symptoms

- Increased blood pressure and heart rate

- Fatigue

- Muscle tension

- Nausea

- Joint pain

- Headaches

- Back pain or other types of pain

How do you get help for PTSD?

It is important to get clinical help for PTSD: it is an anxiety disorder. The trusted treatment for PTSD, supported by the National Institute for Health and Care Excellence (NICE), is currently eye movement desensitization and reprocessing

(EMDR) and trauma-focused cognitive behavioural therapy (TF-CBT). There's more information on both in the "Grief resources" section.

∞

For me, things got better, slowly. My husband was able to drive again so I didn't have to spend my days taking him to and from work, and giving lifts to the kids. Life returned to something approximating normal. I could carve out time and space for myself again. I could give my grief some space to breathe. Little by little, the days became bearable.

Sometimes life happens. And it is unfair and painful and random, but it happens. I didn't pretend to be over my grief at all. I didn't stop being sad or put on a happy face. But my grieving had to take lower priority, out of necessity.

Real life continues, whether we like it or not. We can, and do, endure.

"How is it that the world keeps going, breathing in and out unchanged, while in my soul there is a permanent scattering?"

Chimamanda Ngozi Adichie,
"Notes on Grief", *The New Yorker*,
10 September 2010

FILL IN THE BLANKS:

Today is ....

I feel ....

I see ....

I hear ....

I taste ....

I touch ....

What would help right now is ....

....

....

....

....

....

The worst has happened

Is there any part of you that feels relieved that the worst has happened? In the midst of my darkest days, a part of me felt that at least I had landed, now, at rock bottom. The thing I had always feared happening – my mum dying – had happened, and it was every bit as awful as I had imagined. But at least I didn't have to worry about it any more.

There is a resilience that comes from the worst thing having happened. You have walked through fire and emerged on the other side. Not unscathed, not at all, but you have still emerged, and can continue walking (possibly with a permanent limp).

My rock bottom happened during the month that my husband was injured. The worst *day* of my life was the day that my mum had her stroke and the doctor told us it was the worst possible scenario. The hardest *year* of my life was when I had a newborn and a toddler and zero time to myself. Yet I only truly hit rock bottom when I was in the deepest pit of my grief and had to rise up out of it to tend to my family. Had you asked if it was possible, I would have said no (without a moment's hesitation). Had you asked me in the "before time" if I could cope with my mum dying and my husband being hit by a car within six weeks of each other, I would have laughed at you disbelievingly.

And yet, I did.

You did. You are.

We cope when the worst things happen because what else can we do? We keep breathing. We keep eating. We keep sleeping. We keep walking, one step at a time, in the hope that we will one day emerge from the worst thing. Stronger. Braver. Forged in fire.

A PROMISE FROM THE FUTURE:

It gets better.

You won't go "back to normal", but it gets better.

The moment-to-moment heartache eases.

The sun shines again.

FINDING WHAT HELPS

The surprising physicality of grief

I suppose if anyone had asked me, before my mum died, I would have imagined grief to feel like a deep sadness, a cousin of depression. I thought it was all emotion. I was wrong.

One of the (many) things that took me by surprise about grief was how physical it felt. The frequent headaches that wouldn't lift. The bone-weary exhaustion. The relentlessly high blood sugar. It felt to me as if grief was trapped in my cells, as if the pervasive sadness and despair I was feeling had burrowed into my body and taken root there.

I've since found out that grief and loss are a stress response – a prolonged, relentless stress response that releases cortisol into your system. Cortisol is known as the "fight-or-flight" hormone, the body's main stress hormone that gives us a boost of energy to fight the danger or flee from it.

Trying to figure out how to reduce the amount of cortisol in my system led me to the work of the Nagoski sisters. Emily Nagoski, PhD and Amelia Nagoski, DMA have written a book called *Burnout: The Secret to Unlocking the Stress Cycle*.

"Our physiological stress response is very well designed to help us survive short-term acute stressors, like being chased by a lion. When you see the lion, your body floods with adrenaline and cortisol and glycogen all in preparation to help you engage in a behavior to help save your life. In this case, it's going to be running."

Emily Nagoski, "Beating Burnout" interview, 5 May 2019

The trouble is, we can't run away from our everyday stress – and we can't run away from our grief. So we're sitting with it, day in and day out, flooded with hormones that are only intended to be used as short-term fuel.

As a Type 1 diabetic, I noticed the cortisol the most because my blood sugar was constantly higher than usual (a common side-effect of too much cortisol). Other side-effects are fatigue, irritability, headaches, gut issues, anxiety or depression, weight gain, increased blood pressure and low libido. Tick, tick, tick, tick, tick?

"The Stress Response Cycle is a biological process within our bodies. It has a beginning, a middle and an end. Unfortunately, there's a disconnect in modern human life between what activates the stress response and what completes the stress response cycle."

Emily and Amelia Nagoski, *Burnout: The Secret to Solving the Stress Cycle* interview, 9 April 2019

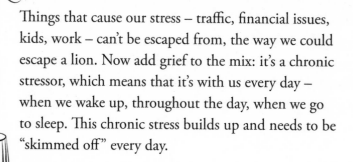

Things that cause our stress – traffic, financial issues, kids, work – can't be escaped from, the way we could escape a lion. Now add grief to the mix: it's a chronic stressor, which means that it's with us every day – when we wake up, throughout the day, when we go to sleep. This chronic stress builds up and needs to be "skimmed off" every day.

Luckily, there is some hope. It's possible to complete the stress cycle – Emily and Amelia Nagoski talk about stress as a tunnel that most of us get stuck inside. But we can follow it all the way through to the light.

Things you can do to complete the stress cycle

1. Moving (any physical movement or exercise)

2. A 20-second hug (where you both stand in your own centres of gravity)

3. Breathing (deep and slow)

4. Positive social interaction (casual but friendly)

5. Laughing (a real belly laugh)

6. Crying (let it all out)

7. Creative expression (of any kind – drawing, writing, cooking, gardening)

What has worked for me is a combination of a few of these suggestions. When I'm feeling at my most desperate, the quickest way to shake off some of the angst is by moving my body. Writing also really helps me (creative expression) and I love a long hug and a good laugh. Then, of course, there's breathing: the most natural thing in the world that we forget to do properly.

> *"If you're living with the aftermath of trauma, simply breathing deeply is the gentlest way to begin unlocking from the trauma, which makes it a great place to start. A simple, practical exercise is to breathe in to a slow count of five, hold that breath for five, then exhale for a slow count of ten, and pause for another count of five. Do that three times — just one minute and fifteen seconds of breathing — and see how you feel."*
>
> Emily and Amelia Nagoski, *Burnout: The Secret to Unlocking the Stress Cycle*, 2019, page 15

∞

What makes the physical side of grief even harder, I think, is that it can feel impossible to stick to your usual exercise routine, no matter how much you know the benefits of exercise. I used to do half an hour of yoga a day, but for over six months after my mum died, I couldn't do any yoga at all. Unrolling my mat, going within, holding poses, silence. I couldn't deal with any of that.

So yoga was off the table. Hiking was mostly off the table because it required too much energy. Walking was okay but unlikely to rid my cells of any deeply locked grief because I was mostly trudging, to be honest.

What ended up helping me was dancing. I've always loved dancing, but once you stop going to clubs it can be hard to find the right space ... Unless you're okay with dancing alone in a dark room with your headphones on (it turns out I am). Dancing without witnesses helped me unlock some of the trauma in my cells. I could thrash out my emotions without having to describe them and – most importantly – without having them creep up on me in a moment of stillness. I could bring them into the light, and into my limbs. I found something quite sacred in listening to my body and tapping into its wisdom as it processed my grief.

One of my brothers said that music was his saving grace. He found an album that really spoke to him and he listened to it on repeat. It helped him unlock the tears that he wanted to cry but couldn't access otherwise. For him, it was all about the words. He would send us a song and then outline the lyrics and how they applied to our situation. I had a similar reaction, but only to two songs – "Hallelujah" by Rufus Wainwright and "Nobody's Fault But My Own" by Beck. For me, it wasn't so much about the words as the way the songs made me feel ... They gave me permission to dissolve.

Whether music speaks to you or not, there will be something that does. Something that helps you feel all the big emotions in a safe way. How might you move, what might you eat or smell, listen to or look at that would bring you peace or release something inside you? We all speak different languages of grief, and that is totally fine. Whatever gets you through the day is exactly what you should be doing right now.

TAPPING INTO THE SENSES:

(some ideas to bring peace)

- Move:

- Eat:

- Smell:

- Listen to:

- Look at:

This is normal

How are you feeling today?

That's totally normal.

Don't want to see people?

Totally normal.

Want to be around people all the time?

Totally normal.

Feeling surprisingly fine?

That's normal.

Feeling like your life has ended and you don't know if you want to carry on?

That's normal too.

There is no good or bad in grief: no right or wrong.

Nobody can do this better than you.

Nobody has the answer.

We spend our lives looking for someone to love: a partner, a friend, a parent, a child. And it is such a rare and beautiful thing to find someone we connect with! To find someone we truly, deeply love – who understands us, who accepts us, who loves us right back.

To have that person taken away is so, so horribly unfair. It's also (sadly) part of life. It was either going to be you or them first, and at least this way you're dealing with the pain and they don't have to. Small consolation, I know.

So, *feel* whatever you're feeling – and allow yourself to feel whatever you continue to feel. The greatest lesson of grief is radical self-acceptance.

Accept how you're feeling right now. And accept how you may feel tomorrow, and the next day, and next week and next month and next year. You do grief the way that works for you.

You are doing so well.

SCRIBBLE PAGE:

Let it all out: vent, scribble, write the same word/s over and over ... Nobody will ever see this.

Sleep

Why is it that the most natural thing in the world deserts us when we need it most? Everyone I know who has lost someone struggles with one thing: sleep. Too little or too much. Not able to get to sleep or not able to stay asleep.

"Sleep is the great healer," my mum used to say to me, any time I was overwrought with emotion as a teenager or unable to see straight as a new mum. And she was right! Without sleep, our bodies are flooded with cortisol, we can't relax, we can't think straight, we don't have the energy to exercise, we crave junk food and carbs, we overdose on screens. It's a maelstrom of bad impulses.

"Sleep is good for you. Getting by on too little sleep increases the risk for heart disease, stroke, high blood pressure, diabetes and other illnesses. It also makes it harder to lose weight or stay slim because sleep deprivation makes you hungrier and less likely to be active during the day."

Katherine Harmon, "Your Fat Needs Sleep, Too", 16 October 2012

"With too little sleep, the body is also more likely to produce the stress-response hormone cortisol. After sleep deprivation, subjects in several studies had higher levels of cortisol later in the day, a time when it should be tapering off to prepare the body for rest."

Katherine Harmon, "How Slight Sleep Deprivation
Could Add Extra Pounds", 24 October 2012

And yet, it can be so hard to get a decent night's sleep when the worst has happened.

"It's said that time heals all wounds, but my research suggests that time spent in dream sleep is what heals. REM-sleep dreaming appears to take the painful sting out of difficult, even traumatic, emotional episodes experienced during the day, offering emotional resolution when you awake the next morning."

Dr Matthew Walker, "Why Your Brain
Needs to Dream", 24 October 2017

Dr Matthew Walker is a professor of psychology and neuroscience at the University of California, Berkeley, and the director of the university's Center for Human Sleep Science. He literally spends his days researching sleep and running scientific studies on the benefits of sleep. He is also the author of *Why We Sleep: Unlocking the Power of Sleep and Dreams* (2017).

Dr Walker has five tips for enhancing sleep – these are commonly known as the "sleep rules":

1. Make sure your bedroom is dark and that you don't look at screens for one to two hours before bed.

2. Have approximately the same bedtime and wake-up time every day, so that your body knows when to sleep. You can't "catch up" on sleep on the weekends.

3. Keep the temperature cool – a lower room temperature signals to your body that it's time to sleep.

4. Don't stay in bed awake: you want to train your brain to think of your bed as a place for sleeping. Read a book under dim light in a different room until you get sleepy again. Or try meditating – studies show it can help you fall asleep faster and improve your sleep quality.

5. Don't drink caffeine late in the day or alcohol before bed. Both of these interfere with sleep.

I try to stick to these sleep rules, and here are a few other things I've found helpful.

Getting to sleep

My problem was always in the "getting to sleep" department rather than the "staying asleep" department. The two things I found helpful (that I still do today) are listening to a guided meditation, and staring at the wall. The guided meditations I love are on the Insight Timer app, anything by Sarah Blondin. She has such a peaceful, soothing voice, and the music she plays feels like it's rocking me to sleep. Having something to hook my attention onto really helps, which is why I like guided meditations that are more like stories.

The other thing I've found that helps me get to sleep, particularly if I've woken up in the night, is staring at the wall. It seems counterintuitive to keep your eyes open when you want to go to sleep, but if I close my eyes there's a whole cinema full of stories and emotions to engage with. By forcing my eyes to stay open and stare at something boring, my brain shuts down and I fall asleep much more quickly. Dr Andrew Weil famously recommends the 4-7-8 breathing technique for relaxation: inhale for a count of 4, hold for 7, exhale for 8, repeat.

The 4am wake-up

This is a common one, although the time might vary. It's when you wake up gripped by regret or sadness or any of the many faces of grief. It is probably the most impotent time of the night, because you're too tired to get up and do anything, but you've slept too long to be able to fall asleep again easily. The only thing that seems to consistently help me is journaling.

My brother introduced me to the idea of daily journaling, and I love it for its simplicity and depth. All you have to do is choose a notebook and write down all your thoughts, every morning. Not for long (10 to 15 minutes) and in a way that is as structured or unstructured as you choose. Just get it all out on the page. There have been studies done about how journaling can help mental distress, and it's one of the things psychotherapist Esther Perel recommends for those who wake in the middle of the night, in the midst of grief.

"When you wake up at night, you write. You write to the one who has gone: you say, 'you know, you've made me acutely aware of the preciousness of life.'"

Esther Perel, "How to Live With Prolonged Uncertainty and Grief", 15 April 2020

ADVICE

Perel speaks about how to talk to your traumatic fear and reassure it. Tell it that you've been through hard things and know how to prepare yourself. "You talk to the part of you that's afraid from the part of you who can reassure it."

The 4am wake-up is linked to things that you can't easily resolve in your head because they repeat in an endless loop. By writing them down, you have to structure them into cohesive thoughts, with a start and an end, and you may be able to find your way out of them. If not, at least you can rest assured that they are written down and don't need to be obsessively thought about any more. Doesn't "rest assured" sound nice?

Sleep is such an essential ingredient in healing, but it can be so tricky to master. With time, you'll be able to figure out what works for you. I really hope you get a good night's sleep tonight.

THE 4AM THOUGHT SPIRAL:

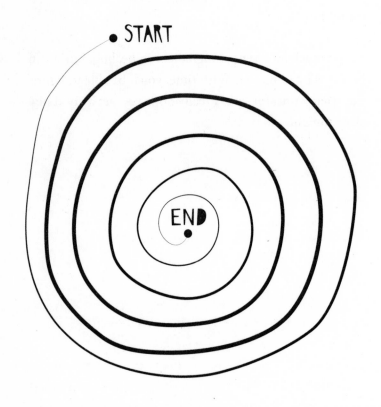

A space to grieve

When you're grieving, nothing stands still. How is that possible? The world continues as if everything is still the same, and somehow you are supposed to be a functioning member in it. The trouble is that if you keep going through the motions without giving yourself space to grieve, your grief will pour out of you anyway – through the cracks. It's too hard to swallow back tears and pretend to be strong and put on a mask all day long. Your grief needs an outlet.

I found it really helpful to create a physical space to grieve. A sacred space where I could go to connect with my mum, unobserved.

This doesn't have to be a big space – it can be a small corner of the room, with a photograph and a candle and some flowers. Or it can be a chair in the garden where you can sit, uninterrupted. Or a few minutes of quiet each day when you get to sit alone with your grief, with the door closed.

For most of us, the mask is necessary some of the time (or even most of the time). Maybe you have to keep it together in front of your kids or at work, perhaps the only way you can get through the day is by not focusing on how deeply sad you feel. But having a space you can retreat to that is all yours, without interruption or witness, can be a relief.

I remember one night lying in bed and feeling like I was going to drown in a wave of sadness. I knew that I couldn't get back to sleep while I was feeling like that, but I also knew that I didn't want to wake my husband because of my crying. So I got up and walked to the lounge, sat on the couch and wailed. It felt like I needed to exorcise a demon, like I needed to get all of the heartache out without worrying about whether I would scare people with the force of my weeping. Aside from the funeral, when it is sometimes allowed, we are not comfortable with extreme expressions of grief – but that doesn't mean they're not there, and that they don't need to be released.

If you can afford yourself a space and time each day to let these feelings out, they won't fester. You need a space where you can fall apart: where you don't have to hold it together so that other people feel okay around you. Ugly cry to get it out. Scream and rage if you need to.

My solution was to sit in my garden, on a special chair where my kids knew they couldn't bother me. It was tucked away enough that nobody could see my face, so I could cry in peace if I needed to, and on calmer days I could just sit and feel my mum's presence.

So much of our lives exist in shared spaces – bedrooms, lounges, offices, public transport. Yet grief is so intensely personal. It needs time and space to be honoured, and allowed into the open.

HOW COULD YOU FIND SPACE TO GRIEVE?

Enduring grief

It can be an ordinary Tuesday morning. I'm working away, crossing things off my To Do list, when suddenly it hits me like a wave of nausea. The sadness is so intense that I'll often say, "Oh!" out loud before I know what I'm doing. It feels like something physical has to come out of me, only there's nothing there but this deep, overwhelming well of sadness and missing.

∞

There are different flavours of grief when you're in the midst of it. When your loved one is dying, it's raw and ugly and heart-rending. Words like "horror" and "agony" don't seem over-dramatic. I remember crouching down and howling in the hospital corridor. Turning away from my dad so that my face could contort without him having to see my despair. It was so inconceivable to me that my mum was dying, so horrific that the decline was so fast, so incomprehensible that there was nothing we could do.

Once we moved my mum home, things softened. There were fairy lights and flowers, carers and hugs, no hospital bleeps, no horrible disinfectant smell, no visiting hours. But she was so much less present, so fast. After we had to start giving her morphine, it felt as if she had started walking over the bridge to the other side. So the grief became deeper. I kept feeling like I wanted to vomit, only it was from sadness, not sickness.

When my mum died, it was all-consuming sadness. I don't think I stopped crying for more than a few minutes for days. The funeral was lovely but similarly saturated with sadness, and other people who wanted to hug me. There wasn't any space to breathe.

And then, back home. Back at work. Back to "real life". Only this huge part of my life had disappeared, and it felt a little like I'd lost my compass. My mum had tethered me to every day for as long as I could remember, a constant touchstone, always there. When I was busy or distracted it was okay, I could function. Yet in the spaces between, when I remembered, it felt like someone had twisted my guts. I kept getting emotional stomach cramps, where I suddenly doubled over with pain. Or I'd get ready to go to a meeting and think, "I'll call my mum from the car to catch up ..." – and then I'd remember.

Seeing people was hard. It was hard to see people I love because they care about me and it was written on their faces and that made me cry. It was hard to see people I like because I wanted to put on a happy face for them and that was impossible to do. It was hard to see acquaintances because, while I could do small talk for a short time, I found it deeply exhausting. It was hard to see strangers because they didn't know, and I didn't know how to interact with people who didn't know because I felt like the fact that I lost my mum so recently was my most defining characteristic. And it was hard to see people I hadn't seen for a while because my first thought was always: "Last time I saw you I had a mum."

It felt so difficult that *this* was the new normal – that this endless cycle of sadness and missing, punctuated by short patches of okay-ness, was the best I could hope for.

My whole life I've worked on myself to improve: spiritually, mentally, emotionally, physically. Now I found myself in a loop where there was no improvement, just endurance. Just passing the days until the pain was less raw, the wound not quite so gaping.

I could see then that it would pass, and I can tell you now from the other side that it absolutely does. While I remember that gut-wrenching sadness and inability to interact with people, I don't feel it any more. Every month is a little more manageable. But I was – and still am – floored by how hard grief is. How deep and painful and hard.

Enduring grief is one of the toughest things any of us will ever do. Give yourself credit for that. Whatever flavour of grief you are currently experiencing, breathe into it. It will pass and another one will come along, and that too will pass. Wherever you are right now is where you need to be. I'm so sorry it's so hard.

WHAT ARE YOU FINDING HARD RIGHT NOW?

Colour me in ...

The wounds of love

When I was trying to find the words to describe how I felt about my mum being gone, I mostly failed. But the one analogy that really stuck was that it felt like a deep, clean cut. We all loved her so much that when she died, it was like a knife had sliced through a limb, all the way to the bone. It just bled and bled and bled, and the pain was so awful that it took up all the oxygen in the room.

But I could see that at least a deep, clean cut can heal cleanly too. I did this weird kind of maths where I would think, "My life has a gaping hole in it because my mum was such a huge part of my life, but if we hadn't been close then maybe it would be more of a festering wound, and that would be harder in the long run."

Can I share a secret? It's all hard.

It's hard if the person you loved was your best friend and now they are gone.

It's hard if the person you loved felt like a distant acquaintance and now they are gone.

It's hard if they pushed your buttons and now they're gone.

It's hard if they were easy to be around and now they're gone.

It's hard if you saw each other a lot.

It's hard if you didn't see each other much.

It is all hard, all in different ways.

The defining element of grief is that there was a person who you loved – not always liked, but loved – and now they are gone. And that is a wound of love.

There is no version of "Would you rather?" that wins here. We are all losers when it comes to love, and that's the way it should be. The pain you feel is equal to the love you feel. It is all hard.

THE THING THAT I CAN'T STOP THINKING...

The story of your grief

There are some stories that shape who we are and who we become. Your grief story may well be one of them – it certainly was for me. I felt like I was one person and then my mum died and I became another.

"Telling the story helps to dissipate the pain. Telling your story often and in detail is primal to the grieving process. You must get it out. Grief must be witnessed to be healed. Grief shared is grief abated … Tell your tale, because it reinforces that your loss mattered."
David Kessler and Elisabeth Kübler-Ross, *On Grief and Grieving: Finding the Meaning of Grief Through the Five Stages of Loss*, 2005, page 63

What I've found helpful is to recognize that the story of my mum dying so dramatically is only one strand of a multi-strand story. Only one strand of our relationship together – my whole life until that point – and only one strand of the rest of my life. All of our stories shape our lives, but we get to choose *how* they shape our lives.

One of the things I struggle with is the erasure of death. Not the actual erasure of a life being snuffed out, but the fact that the death itself (the illness, the speed, the dying) seems to cancel out so much of what came before. I think this must be exacerbated after a long illness because then you have to think far back to the version of the person you loved that you want to remember.

So many people came up to me at my mum's funeral and said that she was a lovely woman, and their best friend (it was a family joke how many people claimed her as their best friend). And she was a lovely woman, it's true. But she was also deliciously spiteful and loved joining in on a family joke at someone else's expense, and could eat ten marshmallow Easter eggs in a row, while hiding from the children. Those are the parts that made her spicy and unique. The general whitewash of death seems to erase out those bits in favour of an angelic version that I find dull and tepid.

When you think of your loved one, what are the bits you don't want to forget? What did they do that drove you nuts and made you laugh? What made your heart sing when you were together? What's the story of your *love*, rather than the story of your grief?

When you think of your life together, there will be certain moments or memories or experiences that leap out at you. Write those down and let *that* become the story of your loved one: the unique combination of details and quirks you couldn't have made up if you tried.

> *"Death does not erase a life.
> It is simply the end of a life.
> And it is a part of a life. But
> it doesn't have the power to
> undo everything a person lived
> through."*
>
> Sunita Puri, "The Uncertainty
> Specialist", *Everything Happens*
> podcast, April 2020

Dr Sunita Puri is a palliative care physician and the author of *That Good Night: Life and Medicine in the Eleventh Hour*. I first heard her speak on Kate Bowler's podcast, *Everything Happens*, and I was struck by her deep understanding of what it is like to slip from this world – and what it does to those who are left behind. I love this reassurance that the way someone dies doesn't cancel out the life they have lived before.

In fact, the way my mum died was lovely. She was surrounded by her family, at home, with flowers and fairy lights all around her, the love of her life at her side and the sound of kids playing just outside. She was there, and then she was gone. What more can any of us ask for?

THE STORY OF MY LOVE:

(These are the things I don't want to forget.)

THE SPACE BETWEEN

A letter to grief

The trouble with other people, no matter how well-meaning they are, is that they don't *get it*. You may have someone very close to you who had a similar relationship with your loved one and understands to an extent, but nobody had the exact flavour of love for the person you've lost that you did.

Which means that no one knows exactly what you're going through.

You can try and explain it, of course, but speaking is hard because inevitably the other person reacts or responds, you can't always give yourself the silence and space you need to get the words out, or you might just dissolve into tears.

Writing a letter to grief lets you say all the things you need to without having to bear witness to a response. It can be helpful to give your grief a name, to try and find a word that captures the mess of what you're feeling (it doesn't have to be a real word). The World Health Organization (WHO) has an excellent animated cartoon about the "black dog of depression" that shows the various faces of depression so beautifully, and how all-encompassing it can feel. In *Like Brothers*, the fascinating memoir by Mark and Jay Duplass, they refer to their shared depressive tendencies as "The Woog". If you have a name for your grief, it's easier to understand that it comes and goes. Some mornings it's a heavy backpack, other days it's smaller and lighter.

Some days, it's hard to remember that you are not your grief. You are currently being visited by grief, but you are not the grief itself.

What do you have to say to your grief today?

A LETTER TO GRIEF:

Who knows how hard you're fighting at the moment?

"I believe we have a sacred duty to live fully in the face of our losses. It's a bitch, though."

Nora McInerny, "It's Okay to Laugh",
Everything Happens podcast, September 2019

Dealing with other people

Oh Lordy, other people. Let's talk about them.

The thing to remember about other people is that they're trying their best. Even when it doesn't feel like it. Even when they seem to say or do the exact wrong thing. Nobody is out to hurt your feelings or make you feel worse about your situation (and if they are, you can quickly remove them from your life).

The other thing to remember is that there is no right thing to say during this time. There are some nice things to hear and some unhelpful things to hear, but nobody has the exact right sentence that will magically make you feel better or – better yet – bring your loved one back.

I remember hearing from an old friend I had lost touch with, who messaged months after my mum's death when she had just heard the news. It was a very sweet gesture, but I didn't feel I could get into it, so I just replied to the message saying: "Thanks, it's been very hard." Her response was: "I'm sure hard doesn't even begin to describe it", and I felt such a flare of red-hot rage that she was trying to tell me how I felt and that my choice of words wasn't appropriate. Now I'm sure, as a sane individual, that you can see that she was only trying to empathize and recognize that it had been an extraordinarily difficult time for me. But there was no right thing to say: nothing that wouldn't trigger my pain.

On the contrary, the friends I grew closest to during my grief were those who were able to be present with me. Just present. Sitting with me as I cried in a restaurant over pizza and holding my hand. Listening to heartbreaking voice messages and not trying to fix anything. Reaching out with a reminder: "I'm thinking of you and sending love. No need to reply." Sitting with me in the surprising boredom of grief, as there was nothing new to say but I had to keep saying it anyway. Simple presence is such a gift. It's a hard one to give.

Here are some things I found helpful to hear:

- I'm so sorry.

- I'm here if you need to talk.

- I'm sending you so much love.

- I can only imagine how you feel.

- I know how much you loved your mum.

- Can I drop off dinner?

- Can I look after the kids for the afternoon?

- Put yourself first – let me know what you're up for.

And here are some I found distinctly less helpful:

- Everything happens for a reason.

  Really? Talk to me about that reason, and please be as specific as possible.

- At least she didn't suffer.

  So my grief should be less because it was such a rapid decline?

- Let me know if you need anything.

  I don't know how to get through the day, I can't possibly think about what I might need from you.

I've said, "Let me know if you need anything" myself, because it feels like the right thing to say. But it is too vague to be actionable – it puts all the pressure of deciding what is needed, reaching out and asking for it on the one person who has no clarity: the one who is grieving.

Having to make any decision at all, as you know, is often too much to deal with, so we go without asking for help because we don't have the strength to choose a person and ask them for a favour. It seems simpler to do it all for ourselves.

I felt this a lot, particularly with my kids. It seemed easier just to trudge through every afternoon, rather than asking for a break. Although if you are able to reach out and ask for help, people are so happy to provide it. They are probably sitting there feeling impotent and not knowing what to do, so by asking for something you are actually giving them a gift.

If only there was a checklist ...

HERE'S HOW YOU CAN HELP:

☐ Bring me dinner.

☐ Tidy my house.

☐ Sit with me and don't talk.

☐ Talk to me about my loved one.

☐ Give me hugs.

☐ Buy me a treat.

☐ Take me out in nature.

☐ Distract me.

☐ Bring me groceries.

☐ Watch my kids for an hour so I can lie down.

☐ Make me laugh.

Understanding other people

There is no pressure (at all) for you to be empathetic and understand where other people are coming from at a time like this. Honestly, the only thing you need to do is get through the day. But it can help to understand where they're coming from, especially when they accidentally say something thoughtless. This happened to me a lot – particularly at the funeral, which is often a hotbed of awkward emotion. It's helpful, if you can, not to get hung up on the specific words that people use, and rather focus on their intention. They want to help, they don't know how, there's no good card for this.

The other thing to remember is that this time of grieving (however long it may be) is all about you. Social niceties and obligations no longer apply. There's no "should" any more. You don't have to see people if you don't want to, you don't have to accept invitations with people you don't particularly like just because they're extended. You don't have to reply to emails, you don't have to answer missed calls (or the phone, for that matter).

I don't answer my phone at the best of times, but when I was in the thick of grief I didn't even answer messages. Sending a single heart emoji was often the best I could do – having to find words to articulate my emotions brought the stark reality of how dreadful I was feeling to life. I couldn't do it. So I didn't.

One of the surprising benefits of grieving (now there's a statement you didn't think you'd ever hear!) is that it quickly illustrates who the most important people in your life are. They're the ones you still want to be around. Grief is like a fire that burns through your life, and many of the less meaningful relationships don't make it through. It's too depressing for them to reach out and get the same response, over and over. And it's too exhausting for you to consider putting on an act. So you don't, and those friendships and relationships naturally fall away. What you are left with are strong, resilient connections: forged in the fire of getting through the worst thing that could happen, together.

Your grief will last as long as it lasts. You may be fine and then totally not fine months later, and people probably won't understand. That's okay – it's not about them. Seven months after my mum's death, I went through one of the worst patches of grief I had ever experienced. It was all-consuming, made worse by the fact that I had run out of my allocated "grief period" in society (which, in case you don't know, is three months). It made me realize just how little we understand about grief and losing someone you love. How we assume, on some level, that the hole closes up after a while, when in fact it may remain open forever.

I got a message during this time from a dear friend who knew how hard it had been:

*"There really isn't much you can do and it's sucky and
sad. I'm really sorry. You keep plodding along through this
swamp of grief, and some days the trudging gets easier
(and it seems you're nearing the edge of the swamp), but
it's all still so recent and new."*

It was such a relief to read her words. It felt like a cool drink
of water to be so understood.

It is helpful to see other people so that you don't get mired
in your grief. Just as it's helpful to get some fresh air every
day. However, choose those people with care – either those
who knew your loved one and understand what you're going
through or, paradoxically, those who didn't know them
and can take you as you are now: an individual without a
missing limb. Everyone wants something different during
the grieving process, so don't beat yourself up if what you
want is new friends who don't go deep, or only a few old
friends who understand your silence. There are as many
relationship types in the world as there are people, so there's
absolutely no pressure to act in any specific way.

One day you will feel normal enough to socialize
comfortably – maybe you already feel like that. Whatever
feels right for you right now is the way to go.

"For in grief nothing 'stays put'.
One keeps on emerging from
a phase, but it always recurs.
Round and round. Everything
repeats. Am I going in circles,
or dare I hope I am on a spiral?
   But if a spiral, am I going
up or down it?
   How often – will it be for
always? – how often will the
vast emptiness astonish me like
a complete novelty and make
me say, 'I never realized my loss
till this moment'? The same leg
is cut off time after time."

C S Lewis, *A Grief Observed*, 1961

Colour me in ...

HOW ARE YOU TODAY?

At least ...

Before my mum died, I didn't know how poisonous those two little words were: *At least*.

Now, if I catch myself almost saying them, I swallow them back.

If your loved one died suddenly ...

At least they didn't suffer.

If your loved one died after a lingering illness ...

At least you had time to say goodbye.

If you were close ...

At least you have a lot of good memories.

If you were estranged ...

At least you were used to not having them in your life.

If they were old ...

At least they lived a long life.

If they were young ...

At least they didn't have to face the indignities of old age.

If they were your first parent to die ...

At least you still have your other parent.

If they were your second parent to die ...

At least you've been through this before.

The truth is that there is no "at least". It is all the most. The most difficult, the most heartbreaking, the most regretful, the most complicated. You do not have to minimize your grief – you're allowed to feel all of it, whatever the circumstances.

"*Plans are made. Plans come apart. New delights or tragedies pop up in their place. And nothing human or divine will map out this life, this life that has been more painful than I could have imagined. More beautiful than I could have imagined.*"

Kate Bowler, *Everything Happens for a Reason: And Other Lies I've Loved*, 2018

BACK
TO
LIFE

Find your therapy

Once the worst of the fog lifted, and I could move through my days without being punched in the stomach at every turn, I still felt … flat. I imagine this is what depression feels like: a constant sense of, "why bother?" Nothing felt exciting, nothing felt particularly fun, nothing tasted delicious, nothing made me feel better. No light. Some things made me feel worse, so I avoided those (yoga, movies or books with any vague reference to death or mothers, seeing people who expected me to be peppy). But all the rest was like a beige slop – nothing sparked any joy.

This was particularly difficult for me because my bar for anticipation is really low. Before my mum died, I would regularly get excited about something as trivial as what we were eating for dinner, or going for a walk with a friend, or date night with my husband. I kept trying the methods that had cheered me up in the past, when I faced break-up heartbreak or recovering-from-illness heartbreak. Yet this was on a completely different level. Nothing worked.

"*Empty feelings present themselves, and grief enters our lives on a deeper level, deeper than we ever imagined. This depressive stage feels as though it will last forever. It's important to understand that this depression is not a sign of mental illness. It is the appropriate response to a great loss. We withdraw from life, left in a fog of intense sadness, wondering, perhaps, if there is any point in going on alone. Why go on at all?*

Morning comes, but you don't care. A voice in your head says it is time to get out of bed, but you have no desire to do so. You may not even have a reason. Life feels pointless. To get out of bed may as well be climbing a mountain. You feel heavy, and being upright takes something from you that you just don't have to give."

David Kessler and Elisabeth Kübler-Ross,
On Grief and Grieving: Finding the
Meaning of Grief Through the
Five Stages of Loss, 2005, page 21

Depression is a part of grief: an entirely natural part of grief. But if the depression never lifts, it may be time to reach out for help.

Where grief and depression differ is that grief tends to decrease over time and occurs in waves that are triggered by thoughts or reminders of its cause ...

Depression, on the other hand, tends to be more persistent and pervasive."

Nancy Schimelpfening, Depression Sanctuary,
"Grief vs. Depression: Which Is It?", 25 March 2020

Don't try to battle this by yourself: you are not alone. You can get help.

My avenue out of this feeling was through the garden. One day, quite randomly, I saw a succulent that sparked my interest. Succulents have always been my favourite plants because they ask so little and give so much. You can ignore them, forget to water them, plant them in poor soil and yet, look! A new baby forms where a leaf has fallen off! Crazy flowers sprout out of nowhere! You can break a piece off and stick it in the ground and it will not only grow but *thrive*.

Succulents have been a bit of a theme in my adult life – I had them in my wedding bouquet, gave them as party favours to our guests, got a marriage tattoo of a desert rose (a particularly beautiful succulent) behind my ear. Any office I worked in, I brought succulents. Any home I lived in was filled with succulents.

This particular day I saw a pot that was overflowing with desert roses. It seemed to be crying out for me to steal a couple, so I asked permission from the owner and did. When I got home, I thought I'd put them in a little garden we have behind the kitchen, which I had tried (and failed) to turn into a vegetable patch. And something about planting those

succulents gave me a tiny spark of hope. It was the first time
since my mum died that I felt I was doing something to
invest in the future, rather than mourn the past.

For the next few months, I became a succulent thief. I
carried a black fold-up bag with me everywhere I went,
and whether it was a restaurant or a friend's house
or a neighbourhood walk, I broke off small pieces of
succulents to take back to my garden. It got so bad that as
soon as we arrived at someone's house, my kids would say,
"There are some nice succulents for you to steal, Mum!"
(Usually very loudly.)

That garden brought me back to life.

∞

Gardening, to me, is the ultimate act of hope. You're
planting something in the hope that it grows and flourishes.
In the hope that you'll be around to see it grow and flourish.
One of the hardest things to wrap my head around after my
mum died was this sense that anything could happen at any
time – that the rug can be pulled out from under us with no
warning whatsoever.

It felt as if an awful truth had been revealed to me, one that
had been there all along, behind a curtain. The ground that
I had imagined was stable was actually constantly shifting. If
this could happen: if a perfectly healthy 72-year-old woman
could be dancing to The Cure playing live in March and
be in a morphine coma in June, what else could happen?
"Anything" was the answer.

The trouble is that if "anything" was the answer, how could I not worry about my dad? Was he going to be snatched from us at any moment, too? How involved should I be in his life and his meals and his health? Did I need to kick into higher gear? Anything could happen!

"Anything" is still the answer. But it's not a helpful one – and in fact, I don't think it's a helpful question. I do think that it helps to understand this truth, deeply, in our bones, so that we don't take things for granted. Health, moments of joy, love. However, dwelling on the fact that at any moment it could all be taken from us sucks all the potential for happiness out of the present, and that's a waste.

If you look hard enough, you will find your therapy to counteract this feeling. It will probably be something practical – DIY, exercise, crafting, gardening, cooking or baking. Something that shows immediate results and also invests in the future. But let me say it again: you do you. If this feels like too much effort, and what you want to do is talk (or weep) it out, that is exactly the right thing for you.

There is a bouquet of therapy options to choose from: one to suit every kind of grief. Grief counselling, CBT (a form of talk therapy), art therapy, music therapy, dramatherapy, EMDR.

For me, gardening counteracted the hopeless feeling by sowing a seed of potential for a long and abundant future. I sense my mum's presence in the growing plants, the butterflies, the resident squirrel, the changing of the seasons. I feel her in the peace and tranquillity I find when I sit in the dappled shade from the granadilla vine, or notice some new miracle babies on my stolen succulents. Something real and beautiful has been born out of my grief, and that in itself is therapy.

Remember: you are living through the hardest time in your life, and whatever acts as a lifeline in these dark days is what you should do. There are no rules for grieving.

Do not stand at my grave and
  weep
I am not there; I do not sleep.
I am a thousand winds that blow,
I am the diamond glints on snow,
I am the sun on ripened grain,
I am the gentle autumn rain.
When you awaken in the
  morning's hush
I am the swift uplifting rush
Of quiet birds in circled flight.
I am the soft stars that shine at
  night.
Do not stand at my grave and cry,
I am not there; I did not die.

Clare Harner,
"Immortality" in *The Gypsy*,
December 1934

Firsts

The first year is the hardest, we are told. And that's true: not only because your grief is still so raw and achey, but because of all the Firsts. First birthday, first anniversary, first Christmas, first New Year's, first Easter, first Mother's Day/ Father's Day/Valentine's Day … The list goes on.

It sucks. What can I tell you? My birthday was two days after my mum died – and I usually *love* birthdays. People kept wishing me a "bittersweet" birthday, and I thought: where's the sweet? It's all bitter … There was nothing joyful about my birthday at all, despite the presence of cake and a movie and presents. I pretty much cried all day (while going through the birthday motions). A few days later, my nephew turned one. Ouch. Then two weeks after that, my son's birthday. And three days later, my mum's birthday. It was a tough month.

Firsts are so difficult not only because there's an empty seat at the table but because it's a marker of the first one of each of these for the rest of your life. Which feels unbearably sad.

∞

One thing I found enormously helpful when it came to the first Christmas without my mum was creating a little shrine for her. It can be awkward if everyone is feeling (or acting) jolly to bring up your absent loved one – some families find it difficult to say their name or don't know how to start the conversation of how much their presence is missed. A shrine solves that. It can be as simple as a photo with a candle and some flowers, tucked into a corner somewhere. It gives a space for sadness amidst the festive cheer: an acknowledgement that someone is missing, and a physical place to sit and think about (or talk to) your loved one.

I've kept the shrine up, next to our dinner table, because I like the idea that my mum can be present for family meals – always her favourite time of day. My kids like lighting her candle, and it's become a light-hearted reminder of her presence in our lives. When the succulent next to her photo bloomed in a wildly extravagant way, I told my kids it was a gift from Nanny (their name for my mum) and they were delighted – and unsurprised.

Colour me in ...

Coping with special days

There can be pressure to feel happy on special days, or to be able to focus on the holiday rather than your loss. Don't give in to that pressure. It is what it is, and trying to feel otherwise won't change anything.

We had a lovely first Christmas without my mum, and the kids were probably unaware of how deeply sad I felt, but that didn't change the feelings. New Year's Eve was one of the hardest days for me because it suddenly struck me that this was the end of the year in which I had a mum, and the beginning of the rest of my life in which I did not. It's naturally a time for reflection, and reflecting on the saddest year of my life did not make for a festive spirit. To muster festive spirit from the depths of sadness feels like pulling water from a very deep well in a desert. I don't think it can be done.

But bottling up your emotions just because of the date is a recipe for disaster: they have to come out one way or another. Better to have this happen at an appropriate time in an appropriate way rather than exploding because someone cuts you off in traffic (true story). There is no righteous indignation quite so strong as that felt by someone who is bottling up legitimate despair and grief, and is then blindsided by an idiot who doesn't know how to drive.

∞

Other times, your grief can be triggered by the smallest thing. One day I felt sad all afternoon because my brother brought us *saucisson* from France. The smell reminded me of a family lunch last year when my mum volunteered to slice up the *saucisson* so she could snack on it before the rest of the family. Just for a split-second I thought, "Oh! We should save her some for when she …" and before the thought ended I remembered.

The seasons changing also broke my heart. My mum died in mid-winter, and as the days warmed up and lengthened, as the air softened, I felt so inexplicably sad that seasons could change and my mum could still be gone. I remember saying to myself, "Next spring will be easier because it won't be the first. Next everything will be easier because it's not the first." Yet in the moment, of course, that doesn't help. All you have is a deep aching missing.

Time passes and grief softens. It sounds silly, but it's true.

Next year will be the second birthday, second anniversary, second Christmas, second New Year's … And it will be easier.

I found it reassuring to reflect, during the first year, that this was the worst the grief would ever feel. I don't think the ache goes away, but it becomes less acute – more chronic. It becomes something you can live with, something that doesn't cause stabbing pain every day. As David Attenborough once said, reflecting on the death of his wife, "after time you accept it more … you recover an equilibrium." Doesn't that sound comforting?

A LETTER TO THE OTHER SIDE...

DEAR,

LOVE ALWAYS,

The anniversary

I did not understand the power of the anniversary of a loved one's death until the first anniversary of my mum's death. I knew it would be significant, of course, but I had no idea how all-consuming the build-up would be, and how much of a release (and relief) I would feel afterwards.

The two weeks before my mum's anniversary were the worst – for my whole family. It was impossible not to think back to a year before and catalogue the train of disaster we were on then:

- This is the day we got the results from the doctor and rushed mum to hospital.

- This is the day I flew to the hospital and thought she was going to be okay.

- This is the day she had the stroke.

- This is the day the doctor said, "It's the worst possible scenario."

- This is the day I had to call my brothers and tell them our mum was dying.

- This is the day the hospice nurse told me what to do with her body after she died.

- This is the day I drove her home from the hospital.

- This is the day she started morphine.

- This is the day she slipped away.

It was a catalogue of heartache that felt impossible not to scroll through, over and over again. Especially because underneath the facts were the emotions. The hope, the rage, the disbelief.

- This is the day I thought we were looking at chemo as an option.

- This is the day the oncologist told us there was no hope.

- This is the day we thought she might regain her speech.

- This is the day we had to comprehend the incomprehensible.

- This is the day my mum died.

By the time the actual anniversary came, it felt like a relief. Like we had been working our way through the worst TV marathon of all time and now, finally, we could watch the finale.

We decided on a mountainside ritual, with candles and flowers and a photo of my mum. One of my brothers and I wrote letters, the others burnt incense. All our kids came, and danced on the side of the mountain to some terrible tween music. We drank champagne and ate snacks and said a few words to and about our mum, and cried. It was beautiful and bathed in a sunset glow, and then it was over.

∞

RECIPE FOR A RITUAL:

1. People you love.

2. Candles.

3. Flowers/plants.

4. A photograph of your loved one.

5. An offering: a letter or meaningful token.

6. Delicious food and drink to celebrate.

Of course, I am not the first of my friends to have lost a deeply loved family member. But I never understood, until my mum's anniversary, how sacred the day is. I knew it was important to send a message during the month that someone's loved one had died, but I didn't understand how sacred the actual day is. I do now, and I will forever.

The friends that reached out to me on the day knew. They understood. If your friends aren't aware, it might be helpful to share with them why it's so important, and what you might need from them. Odds are they don't have the exact day written down, and they would really appreciate you reaching out and making it easier for them to support you. Of course, if you want to spend the day alone or just with family, that's also totally fine. As with all things to do with grieving, there are no rules.

One thing I would highly recommend, and that didn't occur to me until a friend suggested it, is to take the day off work if you can. At least for the first year. No doubt you will be feeling emotionally strange in some way, and giving yourself the gift of time to explore that strangeness however you want (even if you just go for a hike or watch a movie) is within your power (hopefully).

To have made it through a whole year without your loved one is immense. It is a huge achievement, and an enormous sadness. You may feel exhausted afterwards, or elated, or numb. All of these are totally normal and totally fine.

What I can promise is that once the anniversary is over, something shifts. The disbelief lifts and you no longer walk around with quite such a gaping wound. The second of everything is far less painful than the first, even if it's only because you have lived through the first. It hopefully doesn't seem quite so surreal to be a motherless child or a wifeless husband any more. The edges slowly start to heal.

This is a long and difficult journey. You are doing so well.

A POSSIBLE ANNIVERSARY MESSAGE:

The anniversay of my loved one's death is next week: .... the ....

I would love it if you could:

 Join me in celebrating their life.

 Send me a message if you remember.

 Give me a call so we can talk about it.

 Do something fun to distract me on the day.

What helps, and what hurts

Isn't it interesting how much modern-day tech offers us, and how potentially dangerous that can be? When I was going through a particularly bad patch of grief, I found myself slightly addicted to scrolling back to messages my mum had sent me a year before, trying to match up the dates. It became a compulsion of sorts: to see who I'd been a year ago, and then two years ago … To see how innocent I was, and how little I knew of what was coming.

Depending on your relationship, you might have a lot of this kind of temptation. Because I have young kids, I often missed my mum's calls, so I have lots of voice messages from her, and text messages. I have only one 15-second video clip because she was quite camera-shy. I found that really hard to accept for a long time.

Where do you draw the line, though? What helps, and what hurts? Listening to my mum's voice makes my heart swell – and my eyes fill with tears. Discovering her Instagram account again was such a delight, and so hard. Having Facebook offer me shared memories is both heart-warming and heart-wrenching.

I remember watching a TV show once where the premise was that a wife lost her husband suddenly, in a car crash. A friend suggested she try out this artificial intelligence (AI) that could analyse his emails so that they could "chat" over text message – in a way that sounded like him. She thought it might help her grieving process, so she signed up for it. And I remember thinking, "I can see how that would help."

For a slightly higher fee, she could share videos and voice messages, and have the AI mimic her husband's voice and inflections, so that she could call him on the phone and he would respond the way her husband would have. I remember thinking that was a little creepy, especially when she went on hikes with "him" rather than with her friends. Then, of course, because it's TV, the highest tier was that she could order an AI figure who looked and sounded like her dead husband, and at that stage it all becomes a bit unhealthy and unreal.

But, in truth, this is about seeking comfort in our lost loved one who is now irrevocably gone. "Bringing them back", temporarily, in a very small way ... how different is that to me listening to my mum's old voice messages? Reading her old texts? Feeling a surge of delight when I found her Pinterest boards?

In the weeks before the anniversary of my mum's death, I felt compelled to track the journey we had all been on a year before. I read the messages from my mum when she told me about her symptoms and had sent me voice messages because it was easier for her than typing. I remember the alarm bells that triggered. And then, suddenly – no more messages. She couldn't be bothered charging her phone when she was in hospital ... She knew what mattered in those final days.

So I switched to reading our sibling group messages. Reliving those heartbreaking days of disbelief, a year later. It felt like it helped, even though I couldn't understand how dragging myself through it all over again could possibly help. Then one of my brothers confessed he'd been doing the same thing, and it didn't feel so weird any more.

In fact, it felt the same as wearing my mum's perfume. She'd left a half-empty bottle of her perfume behind, and I wore it when I was missing her. I knew it wasn't entirely healthy, so I made a deal with myself – I could wear it till her first anniversary and then I had to put it away. I made the same deal with the messages. I could relive the moments of last year, and the year before, until the anniversary. Then I had to stop.

Modern technology offers us ways to ease the breaking of cords with the people that we love. However, at some stage, I think, there has to come an acceptance that they are gone – well and truly, totally, gone. No matter how heartbreaking that feels. You can't live life looking in the rear-view mirror, even if it feels helpful.

WHAT DO YOU WISH YOU COULD HAVE SHARED FROM THIS PAST WEEK?

INTO THE FUTURE

Bringing the past into the present

There will come a day, in the somewhat distant future, when you will be able to think about your loved one without crying. You'll even be able to speak about your loved one without crying. Won't that be lovely?

I've found it really helpful, particularly with my kids, to keep the memory of my mum in the present tense. I still find it very difficult to think about the fact that she won't ever know my kids any older than they were when she died (how is it possible she won't help me through the dreaded teen years?!) The flip side of that is just as heartbreaking: that they won't be building any memories with my mum because there are no new memories to be made.

The way I've counteracted this particular loss is to keep her alive in the present tense. A short while before she died, my mum sent me Katie Melua's song, "I Will Be There". At the time, we didn't know she was sick, but the lyrics are weirdly prescient. "Nanny sent me this song!" I tell my kids whenever it plays. When we stayed at my childhood home and wanted to bake, I said to them, "Let's see if Nanny left the ingredients for us!" (knowing full well that my dad had not done any baking since she died). My mum was a wonderful seamstress and quilter, and I often point out clothes she's made me, or the many quilts around our home that she hand stitched. "Nanny's so clever!" my son says.

We ended up spending six weeks of Covid-19 lockdown at my childhood home with my dad, and it was surprisingly healing. Before that, I'd only been home once since my mum died, and that had been to pack up her clothes (unsurprisingly heart-wrenching). But for six weeks we were surrounded by my mum – a daily presence in the physical *stuff* of her home. It erased the death memory and allowed us to build new memories suffused with her essence: Nanny's kingfisher who sat by the swimming pool and watched us swim; the mongoose family who crept out in the early morning that she had loved to watch with my kids; the birdsong she used to capture on voice messages and send to us. My kids love hearing stories about my childhood, and there were so many stories to be found – one in every cupboard.

As part of our daily life, I tell stories from my childhood and from theirs that involve my mum, and I have woven her into our lives in a hundred other tiny ways – the shrine next to our dinner table, the photos on the fridge, the quilts on their beds, the recipes I cook, the songs I sing to them. I can hear her voice when I say certain things, feel her touch when I stroke their hair the way she stroked mine. Although they'll never have an adult relationship with my mum, I want my kids to know that she is a big part of who they are, of who I am – and of the mum I've become.

"Life is eternal; and love is immortal.

Death is only a horizon; and a horizon is nothing save the limit of our sight."

William Penn, *NSW Council of Churches Selected Christian Prayers*, PR0061

RANDOM THOUGHTS:

Slices of joy

Expecting to feel happy at a time like this is a bit much to ask of yourself. Expecting to feel any of the good stuff, actually – excited, peaceful, delighted. However, I have found the idea of "slices of joy" very helpful.

It's not my own idea (unfortunately) – I stole it from Google's former happiness guru (I mean, of course I did). Chade-Meng Tan is the fellow, and he discovered that if you look for thin slices of joy – three-second bites – throughout the day, you start noticing them more, and your life becomes more joyful.

We're not aiming for joy right now, of course. We're aiming for a little less despair, a little less heartache, a little more breathing space. But the concept holds.

- A glass of ice-cold water when you're desperately thirsty is a slice of joy.

- A hug from someone you love is a slice of joy.

- Lying down at the end of a long day is a slice of joy.

- Spotting a butterfly.

- Watching the sun set.

- Unexpectedly laughing at something.

- Watching your favourite show on TV.

- Eating something delicious.

- Getting a message from someone you care about.

- A solid gold meme.

- A hot shower on a cold day.

- That first sip of tea or coffee in the morning.

These are all tiny moments of joy, which is all we should be striving for at the moment.

Your particular slices of joy will be linked to the things you enjoy doing. For me, taking a sip of an ice-cold gin and elderflower as I make dinner is a slice of joy. Cuddling with my kids as I read to them is a slice of joy. Sinking my hands into my garden is a slice of joy.

One of the slices of joy I remember vividly is from the week that my mum was dying. A friend had come to our house bearing a box of doughnuts, and for some reason my niece (who was four at the time) decided that it was her stuffed elephant's birthday. I'm not sure how she managed to get our attention amidst all the despair and admin, but she did, and we piled up the doughnuts into a birthday cake tower, found a candle and some matches, and paraded into the garden singing "Happy birthday" to Junior. Then the kids fell on the doughnuts in glee, and the adults headed back inside to attend to our mum dying. But for those few moments, we were all united in the ridiculousness of celebrating the birthday of a stuffed elephant, together.

∞

You'll be able to recognize slices of joy as they slip past you because you'll feel okay for a few seconds. And that's all we're aiming for right now: okay for a few seconds. It can be helpful to write these moments of joy down because they can act as reminders on the bad days that there is actually hope and that you do sometimes feel a moment of happiness.

I should warn you that some days are just hard. Some days I just want to go to bed at 8pm and be done with the day – to press reset tomorrow and hope it's a bit easier. There are days when the fog sets in and wraps me in a blanket that I don't have the strength to wriggle out of. In the midst of days like these, it's good to know that even if they can't cut through the fog today, on other days there are slices of joy beckoning.

Just in case you feel that you don't deserve to feel a moment of joy without your loved one here, let me disabuse you of that notion. Nobody who loves you wants you to be unhappy: here or in the what-comes-next. There is nothing to feel guilty about if you find yourself laughing in the days and weeks following your loved one's death. Nothing to stop you enjoying a glass of wine or a hot bath or a TV show. Survival is not just made up of food and water and physical needs: it is also emotional, and you need to tend to your emotions as carefully as you would a newborn child.

Cultivate your slices of joy. Breathe in the sweet-smelling air. Spend a moment feeling thankful. (Only a moment, I promise.)

SLICES OF JOY:

Beyond grief

To be honest, I'm not even sure I can write about what happens beyond grief because I haven't found my way there yet. Do we ever? Yes, I think we do. I hope so.

I don't think we ever stop missing the person who has gone. I don't think we ever entirely fill the space their absence has left in our lives. But I know we move beyond the fog of grief because I have (mostly) done that. I know we find new ways to cope and survive, even though we didn't think it was possible.

Before my mum died, I thought I had a fair amount of control over my life. If life was an ocean, I thought I had some sway over the conditions, some say in which direction I swam. Now I see that in the ocean of life, I have very little control. I can decide who I swim with, it's true, and I can decide what I wear while I'm swimming – my attitude and approach. Yet I can't decide whether or not I'm going to be tossed onto the beach repeatedly, or if the swell is going to feel too strong for me to stay afloat, or if the waves are going to crash ceaselessly for weeks and months on end. Recognizing the limits of my control is a good thing: it has released me from the myth of my power and into the reality of my true power. What this means is that I stress less about things that are truly out of my control.

I have always been a worrier: since I was a young child. I always saw worrying as a kind of insurance – if I prepare myself for the worst possible outcome, then I'm always pleasantly surprised.

Until I suspected my mum was sick and I worried it was cancer. And then it was.

I worried it was ovarian cancer – very quick, only a year prognosis. And then it was actually oesophageal, stomach, liver and brain cancer.

I worried we didn't have much time left with her. I remember saying to the doctor, "Could we be talking a matter of weeks?" and expecting her to laugh and say, "Oh no! Don't be silly." Instead she said, "I can't say, but it could be."

Ten days later, my mum died.

So it turns out – who knew? – that worrying does absolutely nothing to safeguard you against the future. What it does do very effectively is ruin the present. It takes you out of the present moment, forces you to live through an unpleasant imaginary future, and provides no insurance that your work will come to anything.

In the face of this new knowledge, may I suggest something? May I suggest that we have now lived through the worst that life has thrown us (and we have, and are, every day, by having lost someone we love so much)? Let's focus on this, right now, and try to make the best of it.

We are all in this together: this messy journey of loving, and losing those we love.

I find that strangely reassuring. That in the face of loss, we stand with so many who have gone before us, and with so many who will follow behind. The human condition is one in which grief plays a central part, and that is both desperate and comforting. The skills you are learning now are human life skills: to survive the next few decades, you need to know how to cope when someone you love has left.

Although it seems impossible to you now, one day you will have lived through this. And you may be able to extend your hand to someone else who has just started their journey of grief, and who doesn't think they will ever come out the other side. You will be able to look at them and say, "We are all in this together. It gets better. One day at a time."

I hope this book has helped in some way. I'd like to invite you to return to it any time you need to. You can read and reread this as many times as you like: if you're in the fog of grief, you'll forget it all anyway. This is a marathon, not a sprint, and we don't yet know where the finish line is.

I know how hard it is where you are, and I hope that the way eases for you soon. One step at a time is all you need right now. **This too shall pass.**

Colour me in ...

Cut this out and send it to someone who might need it.

Grief resources

Getting help

Bereavement support
Cruse Bereavement Support: www.cruse.org.uk

For children
Winston's Wish: www.winstonswish.org
Grief Encounter: www.griefencounter.org.uk

Grief and PTSD help
American Psychiatric Association: www.psychiatry.org/
patients-families/ptsd
Mind: For better mental health: www.mind.org.uk
The South African Depression and Anxiety Group:
www.sadag.org

Complicated grief support
The Center for Complicated Grief:
www.complicatedgrief.columbia.edu

Find a therapist in your area
UK therapy directory: www.uktherapyhub.co.uk
Trauma-focused cognitive behavioural therapy (TF-CBT):
https://tfcbt.org

Depression Sanctuary
www.depressionsanctuary.org

Eye movement desensitization and reprocessing (EMDR)
www.emdr.com

Sleep issues
Center for Human Sleep Science:
   www.humansleepscience.com

Professional organizations
Ataloss.org – Signposting support resources for the
   bereaved: www.ataloss.org
Grief Encounter – Supporting bereaved children and young
   people: www.griefencounter.org.uk
Dying Matters – Raising awareness of dying, death and
   bereavement: www.dyingmatters.org

Books
Bowler, Kate C, *Everything Happens for a Reason: And Other
   Lies I've Loved* (New York: Random House, 2018)
Haugk, Kenneth C, *Journeying Through Grief* (St Louis,
   MO: Stephen Ministries, 2004)
Kessler, David and Elisabeth Kübler-Ross, *On Grief and
   Grieving: Finding the Meaning of Grief Through the Five
   Stages of Loss* (New York: Scribner, 2005)
Lewis, C S, *A Grief Observed* (London: Faber and Faber,
   1961)

McInerny, Nora, *No Happy Endings: A Memoir* (New York: Dey Street Books, 2019)

Nagoski, Emily and Amelia Nagoski, *Burnout: The Secret to Unlocking the Stress Cycle* (New York: Random House, 2019)

Puri, Sunita, *That Good Night: Life and Medicine in the Eleventh Hour* (New York: Viking Press, 2019)

van der Kolk, Bessel, *The Body Keeps the Score: Mind, Brain and Body in the Healing of Trauma* (New York: Penguin, 2015)

Walker, Matthew, *Why We Sleep: Unlocking the Power of Sleep and Dreams* (New York: Scribner, 2017)

Internet sources

Adichie, Chimamanda Ngozi, "Notes on Grief", *The New Yorker*, 10 September 2020, www.newyorker.com/culture/personal-history/notes-on-grief

Harmon, Katherine, "How Slight Sleep Deprivation Could Add Extra Pounds", *Scientific American*, 24 October 2012, www.scientificamerican.com/article/sleep-deprivation-obesity

Harmon, Katherine, "Your Fat Needs Sleep, Too", *Scientific American*, 16 October 2012, www.scientificamerican.com/podcast/episode/your-fat-needs-sleep-too-12-10-16

McInerney, Nora, "It's Okay to Laugh", *Everything Happens* podcast with Kate Bowler, September 2019, https://katebowler.com/podcasts/nora-mcinerny-its-okay-to-laugh/

Nagoski, Emily, "Beating Burnout: Sisters Write Book To Help Women Overcome Stress Cycle",

NPR interview transcript, 5 May 2019, www.npr.
org/2019/05/05/720490364/to-help-women-kick-
burnout-sisters-write-book-to-understanding-stress-cycle

Nagoski, Emily and Amelia, *Burnout: The Secret to Solving the Stress Cycle* interview, YouTube, 9 April 2019, www.
youtube.com/watch?v=H2vs84z_qpw

Perel, Esther, "How to Live With Prolonged Uncertainty and Grief", YouTube, 15 April 2020, www.youtube.com/
watch?v=aCP2kKceMb8

Puri, Sunita, "The Uncertainty Specialist", *Everything Happens* podcast with Kate Bowler, April 2020, https://
katebowler.com/podcasts/sunita-puri-the-uncertainty-
specialist/

Richardson, Jan, The Painted Prayerbook:
https://paintedprayerbook.com/category/books/

Schimelpfening, Nancy, "Grief vs. Depression: Which Is It?", verywellmind, 25 March 2020, www.verywellmind.
com/grief-and-depression-1067237

Shear, Kathy, "Complicated Grief Overview", Center for Complicated Grief, https://complicatedgrief.columbia.
edu/for-the-public/complicated-grief-public/overview

Walker, Matthew, "Why Your Brain Needs to Dream", *Greater Good*, 24 October 2017, https://greatergood.
berkeley.edu/article/item/why_your_brain_needs_to_
dream

Podcasts

Everything Happens with Kate C Bowler
Live Awake by Sarah Blondin
Unlocking Us with Brené Brown

❤ THANK YOU SO MUCH... ❤

The story of my mom's death is not mine alone. I'm so grateful to my lovely dad, Raymo, and my equally lovely brothers - Bongin, Smile and Mouldy - for letting me share our story.

At home, Marky, Arty and Ella Bella held me together when I wanted to fall to pieces.

Jessy was my cheerleader from idea through shitty first draft and solid second draft - thank you for being the world's most encouraging first reader.

It is hard and boring to be a close friend when someone is grieving. My most-loved Kindle Club, Becks and Mieks, gave me a safe space to feel all the feels. Squirrel was there, as he always is. Hanli stood ever-present. Cath walked beside me (literally) during the hard anniversary days. And Debbie sat with me through the worst moments, over and over again.

Practically, this book wouldn't have come to life without the wonderful Anya Hayes from Watkins Publishing, the kind of kindred spirit editor dreams are made of.

Lauren Fowler, illustrator extraordinaire, swooped in at the last minute to turn the pictures in my head into reality.

And lastly, I want to thank each of the people I've quoted in this book, for offering some light in my darkest days. And I want to thank you, for joining me on this journey.

Let's walk ahead together.
One day at a time.
Love,
Bridget